FOOD & COOKING AROUND THE WORLD

Italy

Rosemary Hankin

Published in paperback in Great Britain in 2018 by Wayland

Produced for Wayland by Calcium
All rights reserved
Dewey Number: 641.3'00945-dc23
ISBN: 978 0 7502 9688 5
Library ebook ISBN: 978 0 7502 9690 8
10 9 8 7 6 5 4 3 2 1

Wayland
An imprint of
Hachette Children's Group
Part of Hodder & Stoughton
Carmelite House
50 Victoria Embankment
London EC4Y 0DZ

An Hachette UK Company
www.hachette.co.uk

www.hachettechildrens.co.uk

Printed in China

Picture Acknowledgements:
Dreamstime: Pipa100 7l, Alexander Podshivalov 10, 29t, Yurchyk 7r;
Shutterstock: Claudio Giovanni Colombo 17t, Andras Csontos 25t,
Dmitriyorlov 18, 28c, Francesco R. Iacomino 21b, Inerika 17b, LittleMiss 14,
29c, Maurizio Milanesio 9b, Dmytro Mykhailov 5tr, Bombaert Patrick 21t,
Phant 5tl, Sam Strickler 25b, Viktor1 1, 26, 28b, Nickolay Vinokurov 13t,
Vaclav Volrab 9t, Wavebreakmedia 6, Xiong Wei 5b, WhiteRabbit83 22, 29b,
Oleg Znamenskiy 13. Tudor Photography: 11, 15, 19, 23, 27.

Contents

Beautiful Italy 4

Get Ready to Cook 6

Mountain Munching 8

Tiramisu 10

Tuscan Treats 12

Minestrone Soup 14

Middle Italy 16

Crunchy Chicken 18

Land of Pizza 20

Margherita Pizza 22

Sicilian Feasts 24

Fusilli 26

Italian Meals on the Map! 28

Glossary 30

Further Reading and Websites 31

Index 32

Beautiful Italy

Italy is in southern Europe. The country is often called 'Bel Paese', meaning 'Beautiful Country'. Italy is shaped like a boot and has sea around three of its sides. The islands of Sicily, Sardinia and Elba lie off the coast of Italy. All of them belong to Italy.

The capital of Italy is Rome. It is also known as the 'Eternal City' because the ancient Romans believed that whatever happened, Rome would always be there.

Italian food is much more than pizza and pasta. Each region of Italy has its own dishes and ways of cooking. Italians also use cooking methods from different parts of the world. The ancient Italians used both Greek and Arabian recipes. Later, when Italians began to travel to faraway places such as China, they brought new recipes back to Italy. Did you know that pasta was first introduced to the Italians by the Chinese?

The Colosseum is in Rome. It was built by the Romans.

Spaghetti Bolognese is one of Italy's most famous dishes. It is spaghetti with a minced beef sauce.

The Dolomites are a mountain range in north-eastern Italy.

Get Ready to Cook

Cooking is fun! There's nothing better than making food to share with your family and friends.

Every recipe page in this book starts with a 'You will need' list. This is a set of ingredients. Make sure you collect everything on the list before you start cooking.

Look out for the 'Top tips' boxes. These have great tips to help you cook.

'Be safe!' boxes warn you when you need to be extra careful.

Use one chopping board for meat and fish and a different chopping board for vegetables and fruit.

Always ask a grown-up if you can do some cooking.

Watch out for sharp knives! Ask a grown-up to help you with chopping and cutting.

Make sure you wash your hands before you start cooking.

Always wash any fruit and vegetables before using them.

Wear an apron to keep your clothes clean as you cook.

Always ask a grown-up for help when cooking on the hob or using the oven.

Mountain Munching

The region of Lombardy is in the north of Italy. The River Po runs through it. There are also several famous Italian lakes here, such as the lakes Maggiore, Como and Garda.

Milanese style

Milan is the main city in Lombardy. People here eat a lot of rice in delicious Milanese risottos, soups and polenta. They cook with butter and lard instead of olive oil. Local people love to eat pork, which is cooked fresh or is made into sausages and salami.

Lombardy is not near the sea, but fish are caught in the streams, rivers and lakes here. Pike, carp and eels are all used in cooking.

Cheese and dessert

Many famous cheeses and delicious desserts are made in Lombardy. Creamy mascarpone cheese is used in tiramisu, which means 'pick me up'. Panettone is a famous Italian Christmas fruit cake that comes from Lombardy. Another dessert is torrone, which is a type of sweet made with almonds.

The Italian lakes are a popular holiday destination for Italians and foreigners.

In Italy, panettone is eaten at Christmas and New Year.

Tiramisu

You will need:

3 eggs, separated
3 tbsp caster sugar
450 g mascarpone cheese
375 ml chocolate milk
24 sponge fingers
chocolate chips or cocoa
    powder, to decorate

This delicious, creamy dessert is loved by people all over the world. Grown-ups make tiramisu using strong espresso coffee. Here is a recipe for children, which is just as yummy and wickedly chocolatey!

BE SAFE!
• The eggs in this dessert are raw so don't serve it to anyone with a health problem.

Step 1

In a mixing bowl, beat the egg yolks and sugar for about 5 minutes until thick and pale. Add the mascarpone cheese and beat until smooth. Beat in 1 tbsp of the chocolate milk. In a separate bowl, whisk the egg whites until stiff. Gently fold into the mascarpone mixture.

Step 2

Put the mixture in the base of a 22 x 22 cm baking dish. Pour the rest of the chocolate milk into a shallow dish. Dip each sponge finger into the milk.

Step 3

Place the sponge fingers on top of the marscarpone mixture, standing them upright as shown. Fill the entire dish with the sponge fingers, so that they stand firmly side by side.

Step 4

Cover with clingfilm and refrigerate for two hours. To serve, sprinkle with chocolate chips or cocoa powder.

TOP TIP Serve this dessert with ripe berries. You could try strawberries, raspberries or blueberries.

Tuscan Treats

Tuscany is an area with a long coastline on the western side of Italy. It has beautiful beaches and both Italians and foreigners love to come here on holiday. Florence is the main city of the area. It is packed with palaces, churches, museums and art galleries. There are many amazing places to see, including a bell tower with 414 steps and the Ponte Vecchio, which means 'Old Bridge'.

Local cooking

Tuscany is famous for its tasty cheeses, which are made with sheep's milk. One of the best is pecorino. Olive and chestnut trees are grown in Tuscany, and people use a lot of olive oil in their cooking. Local people love to eat beans and a spicy ham called prosciutto. Tuscans mainly use vegetables such as artichokes, asparagus and fennel in their cooking. Many recipes use duck, rabbit and wild boar, flavoured with rosemary, sage and thyme.

Dip, break, eat!

Bread is eaten in many different ways. On its own, it is dipped in rich olive oil. Bread is also put into soups and used in salads. *Panzanella* is a salad made with broken-up bread, onions, tomatoes and basil.

Florence is a beautiful city that is full of wonderful old buildings.

Tuscany has many olive groves. The olives are eaten or pressed into delicious olive oil.

Minestrone Soup

You will need:

8 tbsp olive oil

1 small onion, chopped

2 l chicken, vegetable or
   pork stock

1½ kg vegetables, such as
   carrots, cauliflower, celery,
   garlic, leeks, parsnips and
   potatoes, chopped

1 400 g tin borlotti beans,
   drained and rinsed

2 tomatoes, skinned
   and chopped

75 g pasta shapes

salt and ground black
   pepper, to taste

Minestra means 'soup' in Italian. This soup is made all over Italy, and each region has its own recipe. You can use any number of vegetables and different pasta shapes. Serve with crusty bread.

BE SAFE!
• Be careful when opening
the tin of beans.
• Ask a grown-up to
help you to prepare
the vegetables.

Step 1

Heat the oil in a large pan. Fry the onion until soft, then add the stock and bring to the boil. Meanwhile, wash and peel the vegetables, as necessary, then chop into evenly sized pieces.

Step 2

Add the vegetables to the pan (see 'Top tip') and bring to a simmer. Cook for 20 minutes, then add the tomatoes. Cook for another 30 minutes, then check to make sure that all the vegetables are cooked.

Step 3

Around 20 minutes before the dish is finished, add the pasta shapes and beans. Bring back to a simmer, and cook until the vegetables are cooked but still firm.

Step 4

Add salt and pepper to taste, then serve hot with lots of crusty bread for dipping.

TOP TIP Add carrots, potatoes and parsnips to the pan first. They take longest to cook.

Middle Italy

The region of Lazio is right at the centre of Italy. It stretches from the mountains to the sea. Lazio has an amazing history and the capital city of Rome is here. Many people think Rome was first built as far back as 750 BCE! The Romans visited many places around the world and brought back the recipes they discovered abroad. Many of the dishes made in Lazio are a mix of cooking ideas and styles from different countries around the world.

Farming and fishing

Lazio has plenty of good farmland. Cows, pigs, sheep and chickens are all kept here. Potatoes, artichokes, courgettes, garlic, tomatoes and olives are grown in Lazio. On the coast, fishermen catch fresh anchovies. Mozzarella cheese is the area's most famous cheese. This cheese has a rubbery texture and is traditionally made with water buffalo milk.

Celebrating food

Italians love their food, and they love to celebrate, too. In June each year there is a cherry festival in the village of Celleno. The local people make cakes, sweets and pies using cherries. They also put on parades with a lot of music and dancing.

Lazio has a lot of green pastures in which farmers keep their sheep and cows.

Mozzarella is usually made with water buffalo milk. Today, it is sometimes also made using cow's milk.

17

Crunchy Chicken

You will need:

4 tbsp olive oil
250 ml buttermilk
700 g skinless, boneless
   chicken breast fillets, sliced
   into 18 pieces
125 g Parmesan, freshly grated
50 g seasoned breadcrumbs
fresh parsley sprigs,
   to garnish

These pieces of chicken have a lovely, crunchy coating that is mixed with tasty Parmesan cheese. Garnish with parsley and serve with a crisp mixed salad, tossed in a homemade Italian salad dressing.

BE SAFE!
• Ask a grown-up to help you chop the chicken.

Step 1

Preheat the oven to 240°C. Line two baking trays with greaseproof paper, then brush 1 tbsp of the olive oil over each sheet.

Step 2

Place the buttermilk in a bowl. Add the chicken pieces and stir to coat them. Leave them there for 30 minutes. Meanwhile, stir together the Parmesan and seasoned breadcrumbs in a bowl.

Step 3

Remove the chicken pieces from the buttermilk and roll them in the breadcrumb mixture. Make sure they are coated. Arrange the coated chicken pieces on the prepared baking trays, spacing them well apart. Drizzle the remaining 2 tbsp olive oil over the chicken pieces.

Step 4

Bake in the preheated oven for about 12 minutes, until cooked through. Transfer to a serving plate and garnish with sprigs of fresh parsley.

TOP TIP If you cannot find buttermilk, mix equal parts of low-fat milk and plain yoghurt.

Land of Pizza

Naples is the main city of an area called Campania. One of the world's most famous volcanoes, Vesuvius, is nearby. The area around it has a lot of great farmland because the soil is so rich. The coastline here is called the Amalfi Coast and fishermen catch wonderful fresh fish and seafood along it.

Pizza and pasta heaven

The city of Naples is famous all over the world for being the home of the pizza. Cooks put tomatoes, basil and mozzarella onto a bread base to make a classic pizza. Campania also has a lot of different types of pasta. Penne pasta, macaroni and spaghetti are eaten with tasty local tomato sauces.

Sweet treats

Local people love their ice cream, which is called *gelato*. Honey-coated struffoli puffs are also popular. Zeppole is a special doughnut that is made with ricotta cheese and served on St. Joseph's Day in March.

Simple pizzas often taste the best. This one is topped with cheese, tomatoes, onions and fresh basil.

Fishermen catch fish and seafood along the beautiful Amalfi Coast.

21

Margherita Pizza

You will need:

375 g strong bread flour
1 tsp instant yeast
1 tsp salt
250 ml warm water
1 tbsp olive oil, plus extra
    for drizzling
120 ml passata (tomato sauce)
1 garlic clove, finely chopped
salt and ground black pepper,
    to taste
110 g mozzarella, sliced
110 g Parmesan, grated
fresh basil leaves,
    to garnish

You can have simple toppings on a pizza, or you can add a lot of different toppings. The Margherita pizza is an easy way to get started with pizza making. It is topped with tomato, basil and cheese.

BE SAFE!
• Ask a grown-up to help you use the oven.
• Always use oven gloves.

Step 1

Sieve the flour, yeast and salt into a mixing bowl. Make a well in the centre. Pour in the water and oil. Stir to form a soft dough. Put the dough on a floured surface and knead for 5 minutes. Cover and put to one side in a warm place for an hour to give the dough time to rise.

Step 2

Preheat the oven to 230°C. Mix the tomato sauce and garlic, then season with salt and ground black pepper. Put the mixture aside.

Step 3

Divide the dough into two pieces. On a floured work surface, roll each piece out to make circles 25 cm in diameter. Put onto floured baking trays.

Step 4

Spoon the tomato sauce over the bases. Add the mozzarella and Parmesan. Season and drizzle with olive oil. Bake each pizza in the preheated oven on the top shelf for 8-10 minutes. Garnish with basil.

TOP TIP You can also buy the pizza bases and just add your favourite toppings!

Sicilian Feasts

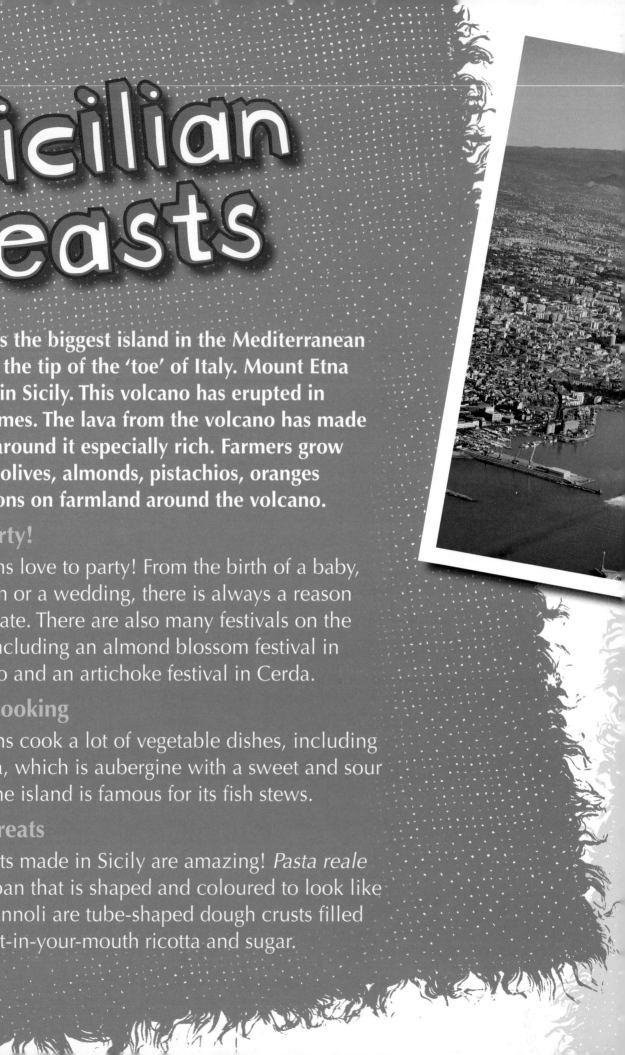

Sicily is the biggest island in the Mediterranean and is at the tip of the 'toe' of Italy. Mount Etna is found in Sicily. This volcano has erupted in recent times. The lava from the volcano has made the soil around it especially rich. Farmers grow crops of olives, almonds, pistachios, oranges and lemons on farmland around the volcano.

Let's party!

Sicilians love to party! From the birth of a baby, a baptism or a wedding, there is always a reason to celebrate. There are also many festivals on the island, including an almond blossom festival in Agrigento and an artichoke festival in Cerda.

Island cooking

Sicilians cook a lot of vegetable dishes, including caponata, which is aubergine with a sweet and sour sauce. The island is famous for its fish stews.

Sweet treats

Desserts made in Sicily are amazing! *Pasta reale* is marzipan that is shaped and coloured to look like fruits. Cannoli are tube-shaped dough crusts filled with melt-in-your-mouth ricotta and sugar.

Smoke from Mount Etna can be seen in the background in this picture of Sicily.

Cannoli al Cioccolato

farina "00" - margarina - acqua - sale
lievito - zucchero - olio vegetale - nocciole
latte - cacao.
€ 1.50 *cad*

Wonderful desserts, such as these *cannoli al cioccolato*, are eaten in Sicily.

Fusilli

You will need:

300 g fusilli
1 160 g tin tuna chunks
   in oil
ground black pepper, to taste
110 g cherry tomatoes,
   whole or cut in half
140 g Taleggio or Fontina
   cheese, finely chopped
fresh basil leaves,
   to garnish

Fusilli is pasta that has been formed into short spiral shapes. It is often sold in tricolour packets containing yellow, orange and green pieces. Here it is baked with tuna and tomatoes, then topped with Italian cheese.

BE SAFE!
• Ask a grown-up to help you with this recipe.
• Let the dish cool for a few minutes before serving.

Step 1

Cook the pasta in plenty of boiling salted water, following the packet instructions. Drain and place in an ovenproof dish. Then toss with some of the tuna oil to moisten it, and put to one side. Preheat the oven to 200°C.

Step 2

In a bowl, flake the tuna using a fork, then gently stir it into the pasta. Season with ground black pepper. Tuck the whole or halved cherry tomatoes into the dish. Scatter the cheese evenly over the top.

Step 3

Cover the dish loosely with foil. Place in the centre of the oven and bake for 20 minutes. Take off the foil and bake for 10-15 minutes more, or until piping hot and beginning to brown on top.

Step 4

Let the dish cool for 10 minutes before serving, garnished with fresh basil.

TOP TIP Choose a harder cheese if you wish, such as Cheddar, and grate it over the pasta.

Italian Meals on the Map!

Crunchy chicken

Now that you have discovered how to cook the delicious foods of Italy, find out where they are cooked and eaten on this map of the country.

Fusilli

Switzerland

River Po

France

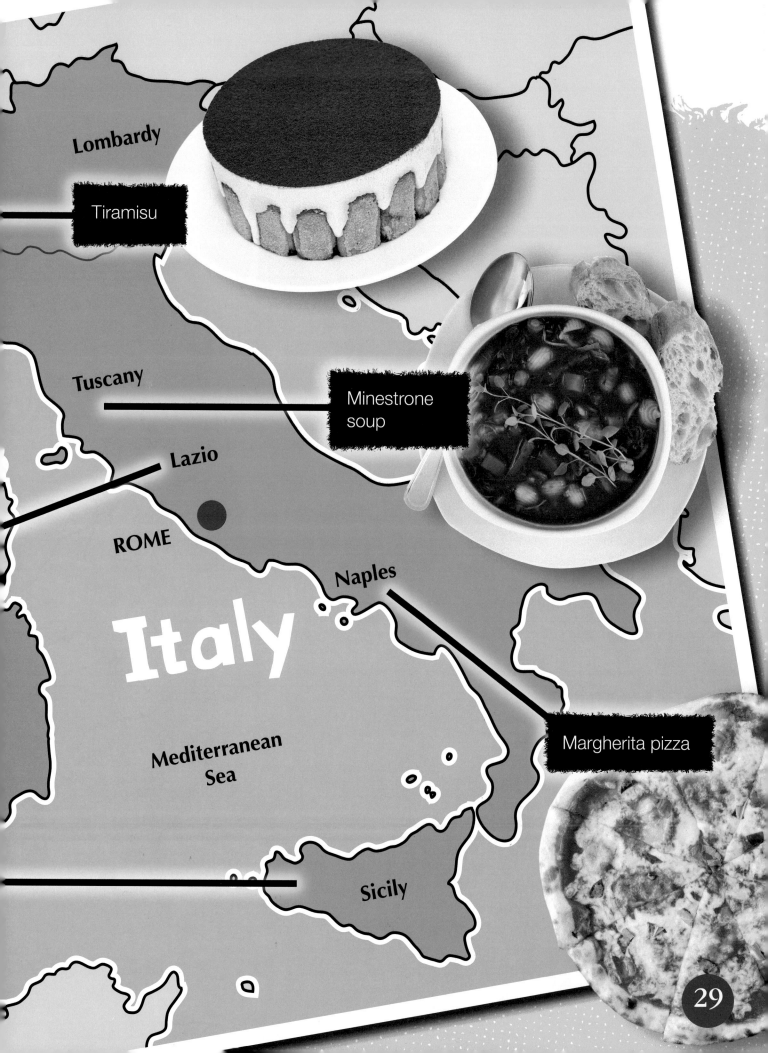

Lombardy

Tiramisu

Tuscany

Minestrone
soup

Lazio

ROME

Naples

Italy

Margherita pizza

Mediterranean
Sea

Sicily

29

Glossary

anchovies Very salty fish that are used to add flavour to salads, pizzas and other dishes.

Arabian From Arabic areas such as Iran and Iraq.

cocoa A powder that is made from cocoa pods and used to flavour food.

drizzle To lightly pour a liquid such as oil over food.

eels Very long fish that look a bit like snakes.

espresso A very strong coffee.

eternal Existing forever.

fennel A bulb-shaped, tangy-tasting vegetable.

festival A large celebration in which many people take part.

garnish To decorate food before serving.

ingredients Different foods and seasonings that are used to make a recipe.

lard A hard, white fat that is used in cooking in place of butter, margarine or oil.

lava Very hot molten rock that pours from volcanoes.

pressed Squeezed hard until the juices run out.

seasoned Food that has salt and pepper added to it.

tricolour Made up of three colours.

volcanoes Openings in the Earth's crust from which lava flows.

wild boar A wild pig that lives mainly in forests.

Further Reading

Italy (A World of Food), Jane Bingham, Franklin Watts

Italy (Food Around the World), Polly Goodman, Wayland

Italy (Unpacked), Clive Gifford, Wayland

Websites

Find out more about Italy at:
www.kids-world-travel-guide.com/italy-facts.html

Discover fun facts about Italy at:
www.sciencekids.co.nz/sciencefacts/countries/italy.html

Learn more about Italy at:
www.ducksters.com/geography/country/italy.php

Index

B
beans 12, 14-15
bread 12, 14-15, 18-19, 20,
   22-23

C
cheese 8, 10-12, 16-21, 26-27
Christmas 8-9
cocoa 10-11
crunchy chicken 18-19, 28

D
desserts 8-11, 16, 20, 24-25

F
festivals 16, 24
fruit 7, 8, 11, 16, 24
fusilli 26-28

H
herbs 12, 18-19, 21-23, 26-27

M
Margherita pizza 22-23, 29
meat 5, 7-8, 12, 14-19
minestrone soup 14-15, 29

N
nuts 8, 12, 24

O
olive oil 8, 12-15, 18-19, 22-23
olives 12-13, 16, 24

P
pasta 4-5, 14-15, 20, 26-27
pizza 4-5, 20-23, 29

R
rice 8
Rome 4-5, 16, 29

S
seafood 7-8, 16, 20-21, 24,
   26-27
sweets 8, 16

T
tiramisu 10-11, 29

V
vegetables 7, 12, 14-16, 20-24,
   26-27